A Beginner's Guide to Drawing Children's Book Illustrations

Written by The Elite Lizzard Publishing Company

"The secret to doing anything is believing that you can do it. Anything that you believe you can do strong enough, you can do. Anything. As long as you believe."
— Bob Ross

Welcome and thank you for investing in yourself!

Let me start off by saying that illustrations are all about consistency and clean lines, which is not easy to do, but if you know the tricks of the trade, you will be right up there with the pros in no time.

The key to mastering any craft is dedicating time to practice. Make it a habit to consistently refine your creative skills.

This course aims to help you illustrate books or other projects. Use it actively, follow the suggestions, and complete the exercises at your own pace.

Some of the lessons may seem silly, but professionals use them to warm up for illustrations.

If you don't have the latest computer or a big budget for software, here are some free programs with a small footprint for your computer or tablet. Consider getting a drawing tablet, like a Wacom, which is affordable and can enhance your practice using techniques from this course. Wacom tablets often cost around $100 but keep an eye out for sales on Amazon.

BEST FREE Illustration programs:

1. Krita- highly recommended and personally used. Krita | Digital Painting. Creative Freedom.
2. Inkscape- Very decent program. Draw Freely | Inkscape
3. Sketchpad- It works, but it's not the best.

There are others but I think these rank in the top two free sites and I have used both and can say with confidence that they are decent to get you well on your way to illustrating your book. Krita also has a great option for keeping straight lines. You will definitely want to utilize it.

Using the basic size 5 opacity brush click on it and remove all the stuff off of it, this is called flow pressure. Uncheck every little thing, then leave size on. Go to brush tip and go to auto and make sure it is clicked on. This will give you perfect lines. Not sure of what I mean? Find great tutorials on YouTube videos and it will show you how to do it. <u>Look up : How to get 100% SMOOTH LINES in Krita (Fix Jagged Edges) - YouTube</u>

For Inkscape Search a quick way it shows you how to get smooth lines. <u>Interactive smooth lines for Inkscape- YouTube.</u>

If you have the money to invest in a drawing application, choose Adobe Photoshop! It is by far one of the best paid drawing applications. If you have an apple drawing tablet then I would advise Procreate. But again, look into it and do your research to see pros and cons of them.

***

About Your Teacher

I want to provide some background information on my qualifications and experience. My name is Lizy Campbell, and I reside in Canada. I have illustrated well over 50 books and am a self-taught artist. Initially, I started as a pet portrait artist and completed over a hundred paintings from my home before being commissioned to illustrate a children's book. At that time, I was raising two special needs children alone and working another job.

Despite my initial apprehension about illustrating, I decided to proceed and was pleased with the outcome. To further my skills, I taught myself how to use the Adobe Photoshop application through an online course and watching many YouTube videos. Subsequently, I sought out publishers looking for illustrators, found a company in the USA, and collaborated with them for over four years, gaining knowledge about publishing and taking additional courses to improve my skills. I continued to practice and refine my abilities to create books for others.

Currently, I am an author myself and the owner of The Elite Lizzard Publishing Company, which has over 20 authors within three years of its establishment. This journey I wanted to share with you highlights the importance of pursuing one's dreams with dedication and passion. If I can do it, so can you!

***

Illustrating children's books combines artistic skills with storytelling. As an illustrator, you have the role of visualizing stories, engaging young readers, and contributing to their interest in books. This profession can also offer opportunities to earn a substantial income. This guide provides essential tips and strategies on how to make money by illustrating children's books, as well as improving your artistic skills to become a successful professional illustrator.

LET'S BEGIN!

Drawing figures

Let's delve into the basics of drawing. Character placement is the method by which your character depicts movement. It should maintain consistency and flow with your illustrations throughout your book.

PRACTICE. PRACTICE. PRACTICE.

Before you start, try warming up and getting familiar with your tablet you are using by drawing a series of quick circles, and even lines. The faster you do it the better the circle or the line will get.

This is something you should do every time you get ready to draw, warming up the muscles in your hand by creating loose circles and a series of straight lines. This will help when you start actual drawing. Use this book to draw as well. Although we spend a lot of time on digital tablets, hand drawing should never be ignored. In fact, I encourage you to draw daily with a pencil to better perfect your skill level.

Your Practice Exercise: Practice making a series of circles fast using your wrist. The more you do the better the circles will start to come together.

Doing this slowly will not help you form the muscle movement needed to draw circles quickly. Try making a circle slow and then fast and see the difference. By going faster, we have crisper circles. This applies to straight lines as well, the slower you try to create a straight line, the more wiggles and imperfections show up. Remember, this is a learned skill, so it will take time to get the hang of things.

"Talent is a pursued interest. Anything that you're willing to practice, you can do." — Bob Ross

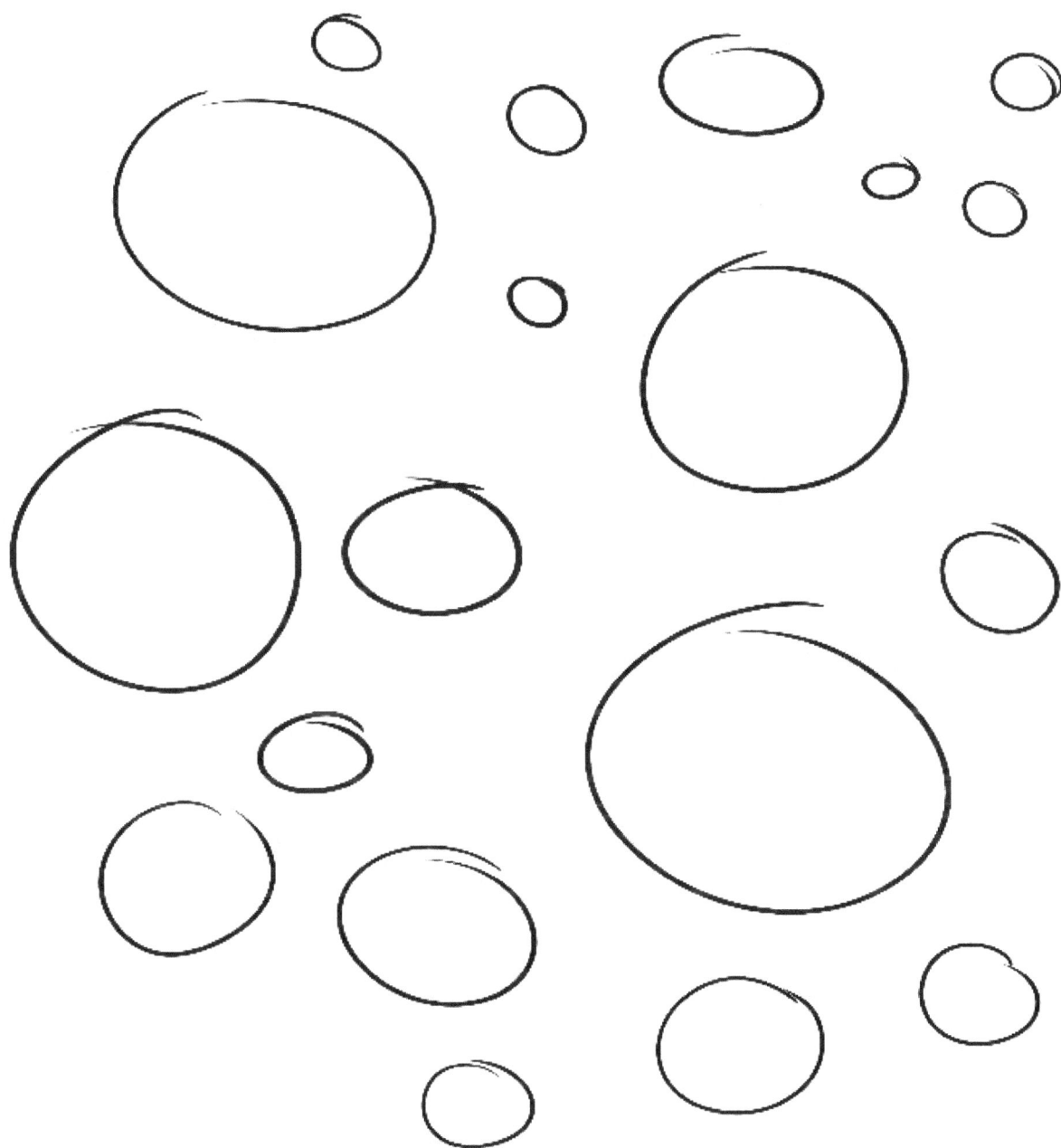

Practice Pages for hand drawing

CHARACTER FIGURE DRAWINGS

To effectively draw figures lets break the components down into shapes. Here is a super quick example of the shapes that have been broken down in a character.

See how I am using those circles now? We can simplify our initial drawing, freeing us up to play with stances and then form those details later.

By using shapes to build a character's body we can break it down into more manageable sections.

You can also distort your characters image by exaggerating certain aspects of them to create fun loving characters for your book. Try experimenting on your own creating exaggerated figures either shortening the upper half of the body or elongating it. Make it fatter or super skinny to produce unique figures of your own for your story. Here are a few examples I have provided for you to see what I mean.

This idea can be applied to various single components also, larger head and regular body, small head larger body, large feet, etc. Play around with it and you end up with a unique character that will make children laugh. You want to have a sense of whimsy; children have avid imaginations, and we want to connect everything together by adding items that are common.

Your Practice Exercise: Practice making various figures both in normal and exaggerated forms. Use the circles as shapes to help you understand and transform the bodies proportions.

Practice pages

The Unspoken Drawing Rule

A key guideline for creating dynamic illustrations is to include three objects or an odd number of elements in the composition. Additionally, avoid making both sides of a character's pose identical.

So, lets break that down further for explanation. If you are planning to put flowers, trees, or anything like this you need to keep in mind the odd rule. Do not put things evenly so if you have 1 tree, this is impressive, 2 exact trees no. 3 is a yes, ok! 4, no, and so on.

Flowers, and accessories, all of it should be remembered to be odd in number as well. This creates more interest. Our eyes look for similarities, so we want to try and keep the eye moving, but our main focus is the character.

For the positioning of a character, do not put one arm the same position as the other, legs too. Always have one slightly turned, one hand up one in a pocket or holding an object for example. Your eyes will not be able to pick out any similarities.

This is the illustrator rule of thumb. Hair is the same, have one side be over the shoulder while the other side is flipped back possibly. The main goal is to keep it interesting.

Some of the top illustrators apply this rule and they are so good that you will not even notice it. But you will be looking for it now and you will find it.

Another fun fact for drawing on your tablet, do not be afraid to move your image around, throw it upside down to get those lines right, use it as if it were a piece of paper and zoom in and out. I recommend zooming in close to get the lines perfect but zoom to full page to have a look at what you are doing every so often. Having different views helps us to gain a better perspective.

Your Practice Exercise: Go to the site Artstation or Behance to check this principal. See if you can spot those rules of three and positioning in character drawings and backgrounds.

EYES

Eyes in your characters drawing are especially important, and this is where you really want to consider what you are trying to show. Eyes in cartoons can have various typical looking types or you may opt for a unique design. Please take some time to fine tune your eyes on your character and remember once you decide on the eyes try to incorporate that with all the remaining characters as it sets the tone for the style and an overall polished look of characters.

What do I mean? *Please look up the following cartoons to understand* they idea behind what I am saying. Smurfs, The Simpsons, Family Guy. The Flintstones. See the theme?

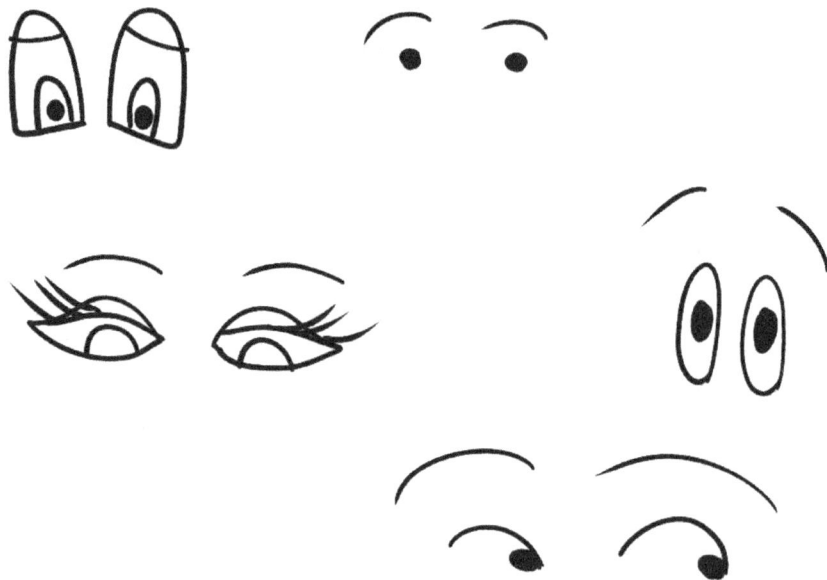

It is essential to ensure the characters you create are consistent yet possess unique individual traits. By adhering to this foundational principle, you will recognize the significance of cohesive facial features in character design. Here are a few examples of different eye shapes you can play around with that are classics. (See the Illustration on the previous page).

You might be thinking why did she start off with figures first and not eyes? Because I want to get all the stuff you think is daunting out of the way so we can start getting into the real thick of it. This is me skimming over a few things before I start getting into more details. I want you to think of this not in terms of something hard to do, but a learning and fun experience.

As I go along, I will go back into the characters design elements in even more detail. But for now, I want you to understand the whole package of creating a character by breaking it down into simple terms and then building it up to more.

Your Practice Exercise: Try practicing drawing a series of eyes. Assorted styles and shapes. Try to make both eyes as similar as possible. This is not as easy as it sounds. Good Luck!

Use these practice pages to draw some eyes by hand!

COLOUR

Colour is another major component to consider before starting your journey into character building and worlds.

Some of the best children's books are loud and full of color, but in a way that to kids and even adults think it's all bright, but that's not the case.

You see the illustrator wants you to focus on the character being presented, so how do they do this?

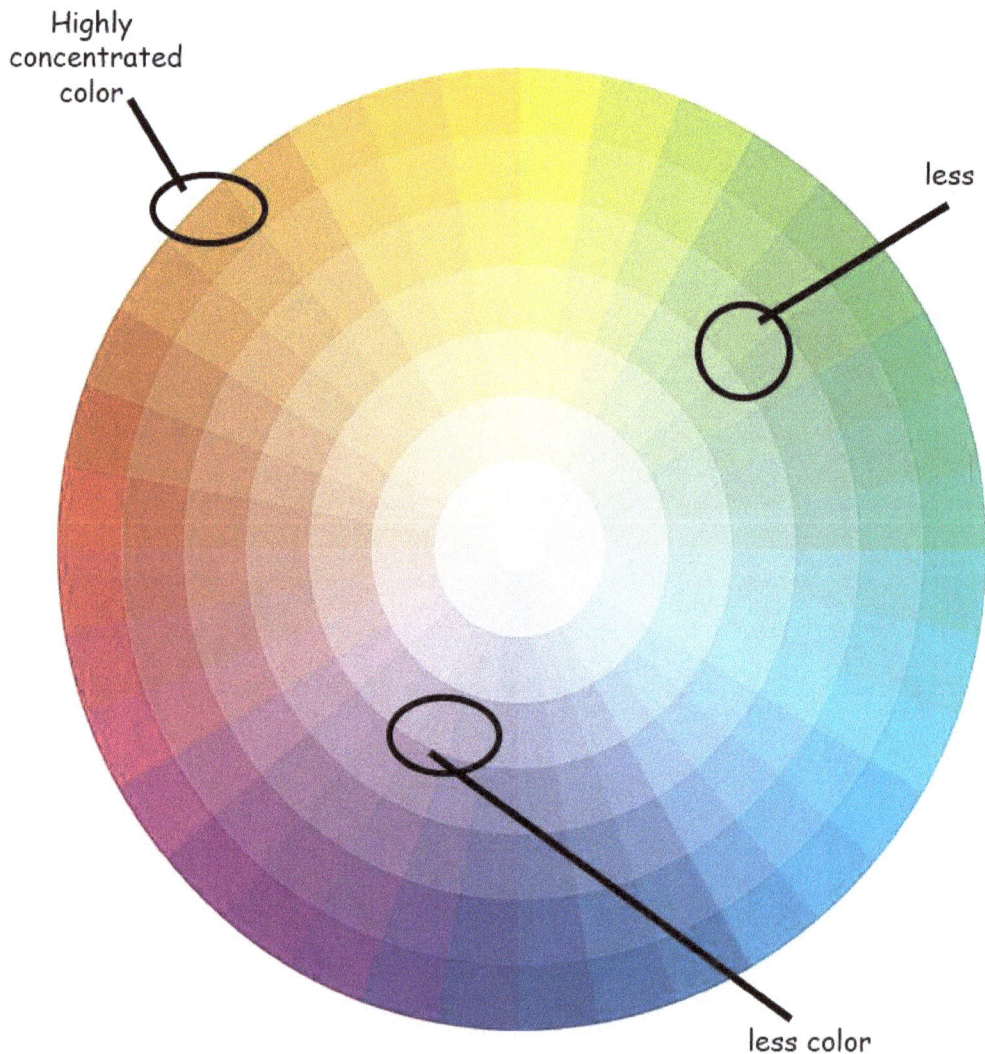

Highly concentrated color

less

less color

By muting the surrounding colour's to make the main one to stand out. And now you are thinking, how? Well, on the colour wheel we see various degrees of the same color. *(See previous page illustration).*

This is how the artist keeps the colors bright but not as bright as our main characters.

The background is usually where a lot of this takes place. Keeping it all bright and whimsical but colour saturation is not the same. Now you learned a trick that illustrators use.

Now let's choose your colour palette. Matching complementary colour's beforehand saves time and keeps illustrations polished and well-designed. You should always ask the author what colour pallet they prefer before diving into the colouring portion of illustrations.

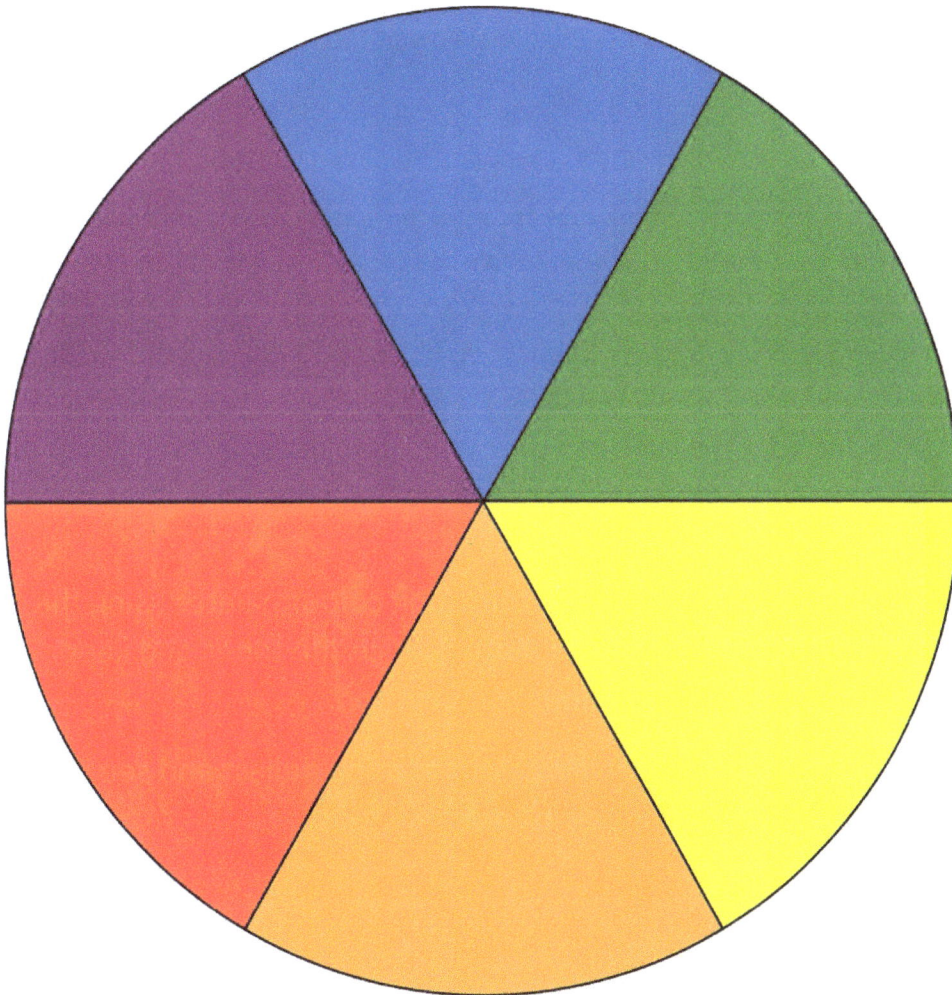

Colour Meanings:

- **Green**: Balance, Harmony, Love, Communication, Social, Nature, Acceptance

- **Blue-Indigo**: Calmness, Peace, Love, Honesty, Kindness, Truth, Inner Peace, Emotional Depth, Devotion

- **Violet**: Intuition, Imagination, Universal Flow, Meditation, Artistic Qualities

- **Red**: Physical Energy, Vitality, Stamina, Grounding, Spontaneity, Stability, Passion

- **Orange**: Creativity, Productivity, Pleasure, Optimism, Enthusiasm, Emotional Expression

- **Yellow**: Fun, Humor, Lightness, Personal Power, Intellect, Logic, Creativity

Take a minute to look over the colors that are used in therapy. Using the colour wheel on your program you will notice that it also knows the colour's in which you are using that match if you go along in one section all the way around you will have consistent colour, and all match each other. Going outside of that will change the range of saturation and overall match.

All these colour's have great meaning so you can create with those main ones to set the tone of what you want the reader to feel while they look at the illustrations. Something to think about then creating your book.

Your Practice Exercise: Try making a matching colour palette using the same row of colour all around the sphere. Notice the tones and keep the same areas to create a unison colour combination.

*Create one for the most saturated colour's to the dullest and see how they automatically look like they are all in the same tone.

For hand drawing, use one colouring pencil pressing hardest on the outside and gradually getting lighter in the first circle. In the second circle find three pencil crayons all in the same range and put lightest to darkest.

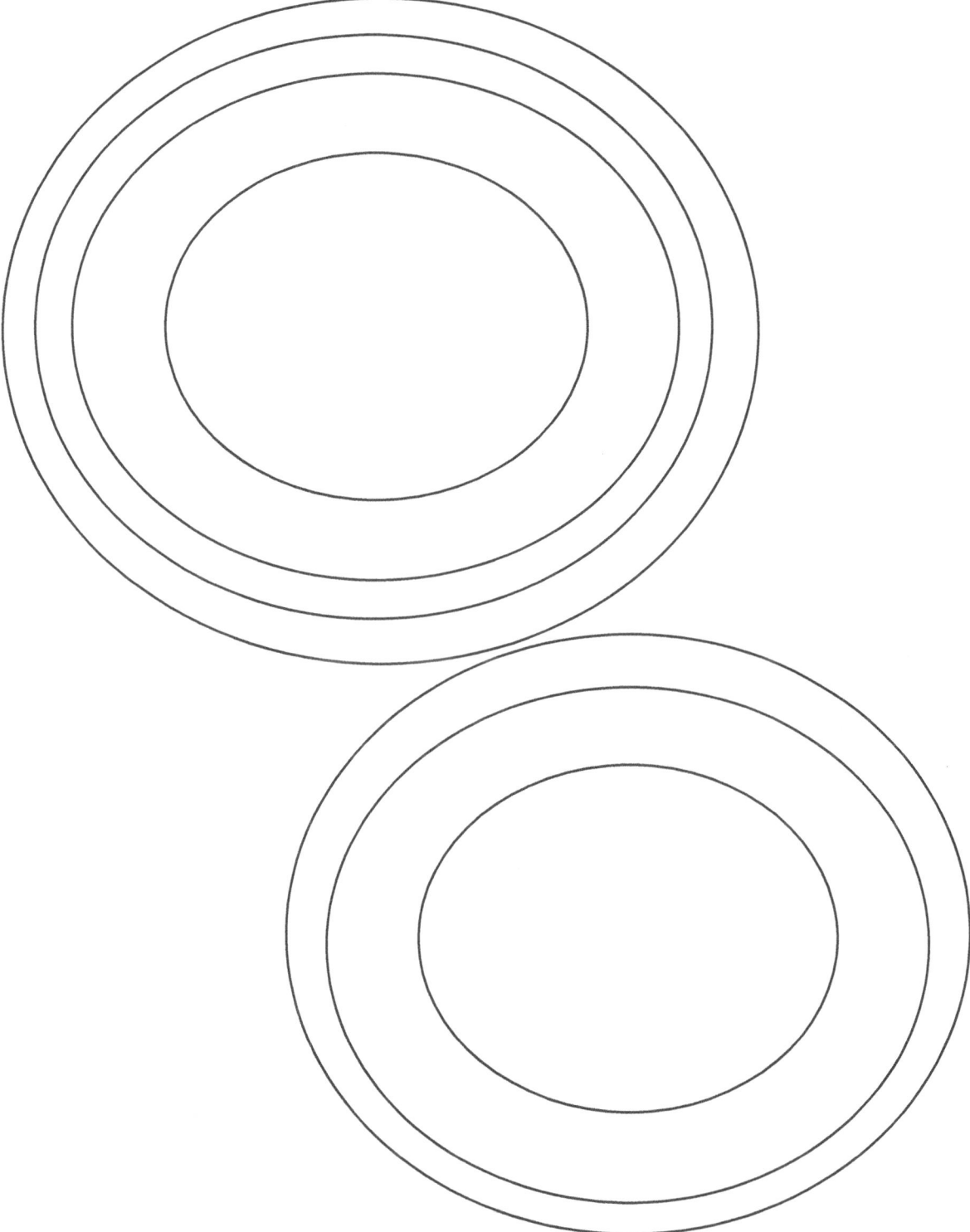

Backgrounds

When we draft a story for kids, we imagine the world in which they would like to live in. Either it's a common place, or a fantasy. Creating this world for kid's to enjoy is to still have identifiable components with the surroundings to help ground the illustration. We also want to help their imagination, which is important, so adding in imaginary fun elements brings the drawing all together.

FOR TABLET AND DIGITAL ART:

We can create images separately by first designing the character, then adding it on a separate layer over the background. This method saves time and ensures consistency if the scene stays the same while the character changes.

Make sure that the colour is not as saturated in the background as the character. That means going down two grades of colour saturation which still makes it nice and bright, doing this does not overwhelm the child with distraction from the story being illustrated. Remember our character is the most important component on the page.

For Drawing illustrations, lightly sketch out the layout before investing in the final copy of your illustration to ensure placement is optimal and you will usually have to verify this with the author, so no coloring is needed yet.

Trees can be easy or hard and are quite common to draw it just depends on you and what overall look you want. A wonderful trick if you want leaves is to make a random pile of leaves and colour it then copying it and rotating the image so that it does not look stamped on. Here is an example;

cluster of leaves

-Without me touching it up, you can see how I used that same cluster of leaves I created to make a whole tree, and it was quite fast to do.

FOR TABLET ART:

Exercise: Try making a bunch of leaves in a cluster and then cloning them using the quick selection tool or use the instructions below if using Krita or Inkscape and then rotate the cluster of leaves to make a tree of leaves as shown in the example above.

*The clone tool is a brush type in **Krita,** so open the brush editor from the top toolbar and select duplicate. How do I select and duplicate in Krita? Common Shortcuts while Using Selections Copy – **Ctrl + C or Ctrl + Ins**. Paste – Ctrl + V or Shift + Ins. Cut – Ctrl + X, Shift + Del. Copy from All Layers – Ctrl + Shift + C.

*Inkscape: Copy and paste in Inkscape to see which one fits best in each situation. 1. Duplicate Go ahead and select an object to duplicate. Either head up to Edit > Duplicate or simply hit Control-D to do so.

"There's nothing wrong with having a tree as a friend."
— Bob Ross

Your Practice Exercise for hand drawing: Try to create a bunch of unique looking trees using various shapes or cartoon clouds to give different ideas to your illustrations. This practice exercise will help you create your own style.

Practice pages

PERSPECTIVES

Getting the right angle and perspective takes practice. I use a ruler for this to help as a guide for the angles I wish to achieve.

Here is a simplified view of different angles of drawings to help you remember when doing your own illustration.

Playing around with different angles will help you achieve the best results; I would even set your rulers first on your drawing with linework in its own layer that you can remove once you have achieved the angles for your drawing digitally. Putting these mock lines as a guide will also help to keep you from veering off course.

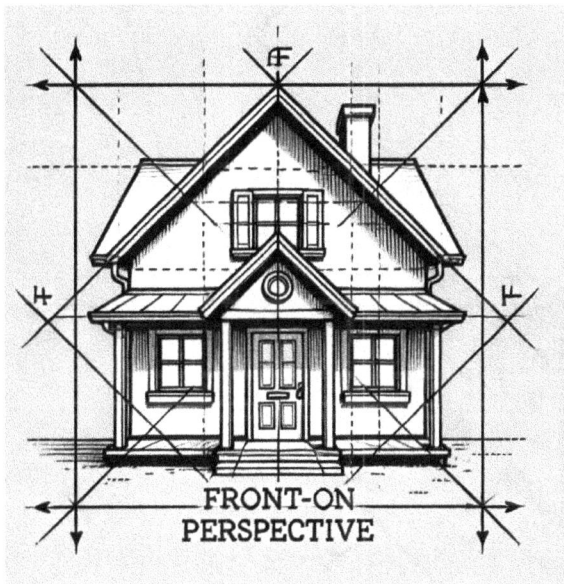

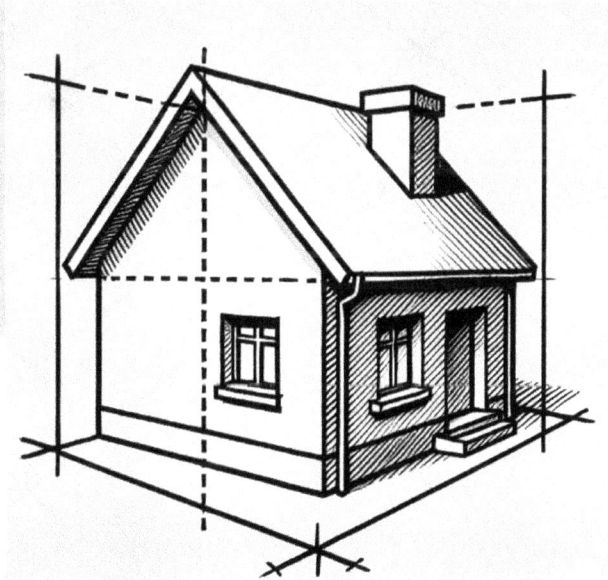

FRONT-ON PERSPECTIVE

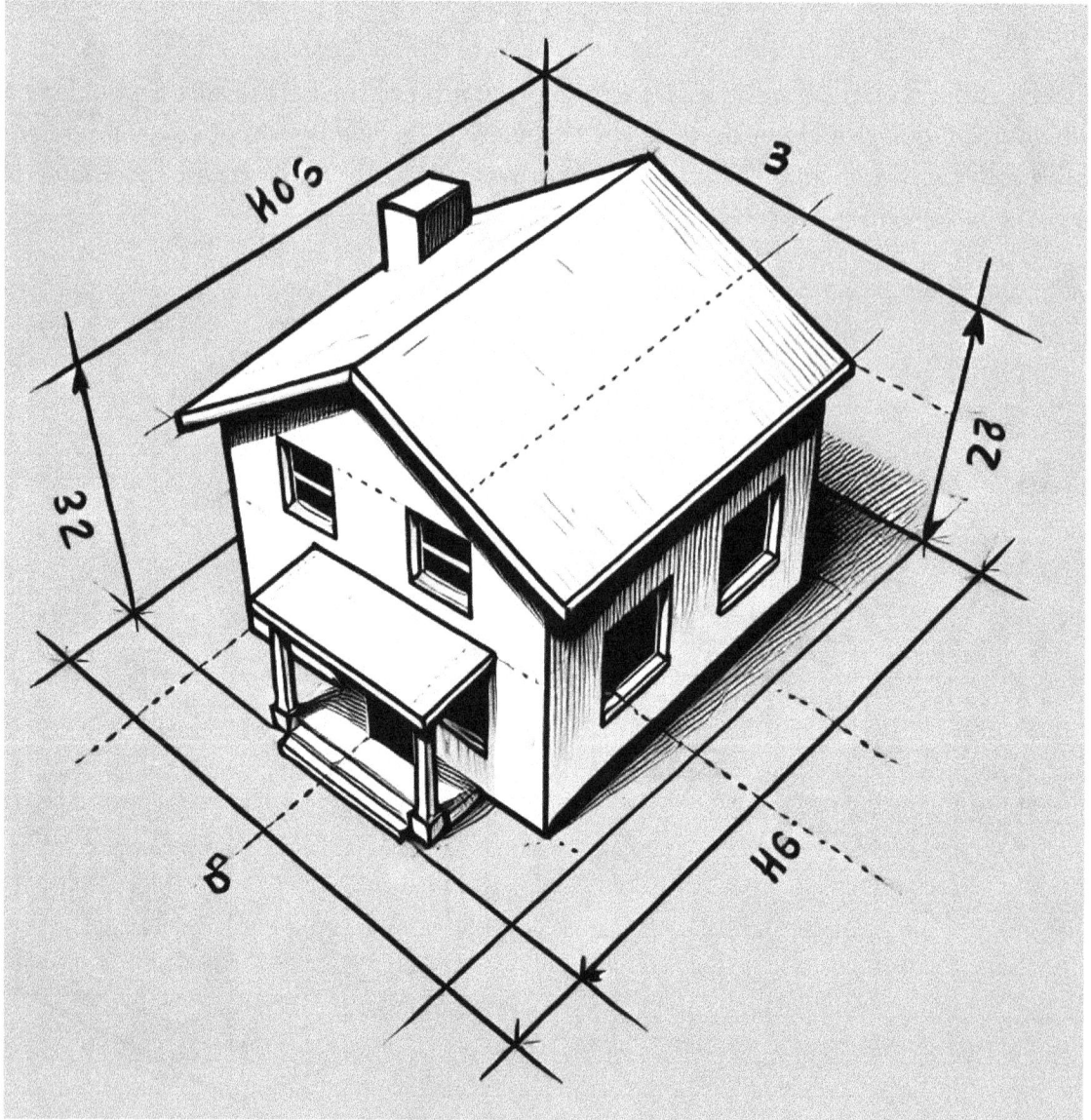

Your Practice Exercise: Try to recreate a house using one or more of the angles shown, add details and doors with the same angles as the house. You will notice that you really must pay attention to the eye line here to make sure everything flows together.

**Do a rough draft sketch and then finished one on the next page.

Sketch here:

Good draft:

Drawing heads

You may or may not have heard of the Loomis method for drawing heads accurately. This technique helps you to be able to draw heads precisely at any angle.

This exercise is if you are looking to create more realistic character. Some parents ask for their child to be in the story or other members of the family, so this can help you, should you come across this with a client.

Step one: Draw a circle

Step two: Once we have the circle drawn, we draw in a line through the vertical center of the face, which will represent the line where we will draw the nose. We will also draw a horizontal line through the ball, representing the eyebrow line. Together these lines form a cross and are of utmost importance to getting the Loomis construction right.

Step three: We need to establish a flat side where the placement of the ear will be which will also determine where the person is looking and what angle we are trying to achieve.

Now we can see where the ear will be and in what direction the face will be. There are tutorials I have used to get me started on practicing this method which I think you will find helpful. Once you get the hang of it you will not even think about this entire process. Look up on YouTube: How to quickly draw Loomis heads

Honestly, this is the best method for accuracy of head drawings but remember you can exaggerate the nose or whatever you like once you get the basics down. For the rest of the body, I would suggest purchasing a figure drawing wooden model. They can be purchased cheaply; I have even seen them at the Dollar store on occasion.

There are countless videos on YouTube to help you perfect your drawings using the Loomis technique as well, so don't be afraid to click many to find one that resonates with you.

Your Practice Exercise: Practice creating heads of different angles using the Loomis method. Create the eyes and placement of nose to get accurate faces.

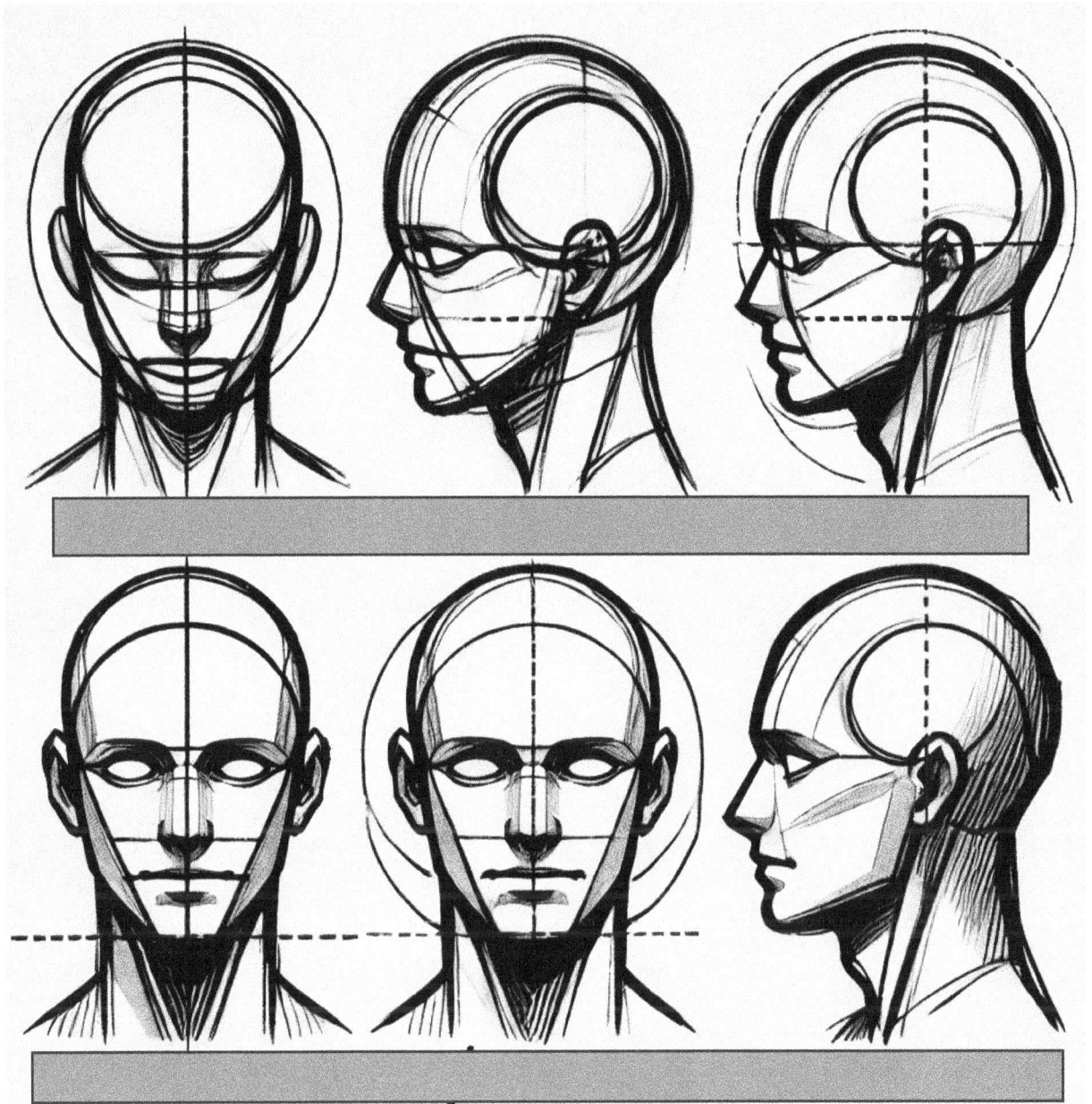

Practice pages

Facial expressions

This is an important part of your characters overall appearance. So, now you know how to draw dynamic heads, it's time to get to practicing a character's facial expressions. This is an extremely important part of drawing to really emphasis more of the story to telling a reader.

This takes practice to be able to have consistency in the characters features, no matter what the mood is. Like I have said all along, to get better at working that creative muscle you need to **practice.** So, practice all the emotions your character could potentially have.

Let us start with the basics, mad, happy, sad.

I am going to demonstrate simple faces to give you an example, this is something you should do to go a little beyond as characters are quite animated.

*As you can see even the bow in her hair is reflecting the sadness, its droopy.

*You could even make her happier by opening her mouth even more.

Your Practice Exercise: Create your own character using only the heads to demonstrate different expressions or feelings of the character. Practicing either by using your tablet or hand drawing this will help to perfect your characters appearance for when you begin illustrating your book.

Practice Pages

Character Movement

Showing a character who is moving fast is not always easy but there are tricks for this. Blurring the background is one way. Another is to make the character look as though it is

in movement by showing outlines of its legs. Here is what I mean:

What is done here is showing the feet running in movement by lightly copying the initial cat multiple times. By copying and pasting it and using the opacity set to less than 50% so you can see it but not as much as the final movement of the animal.

Another way to create the effect of a fast-moving cat, blur the background first and add the characters later. Use a soft brush to add white for a sense of speed. Both techniques effectively show movement. This is a digital exercise I encourage you to practice.

Your Practice Exercise: Practice your character running using one the examples shown to create movement on your digital tablet. Practice this again using your hand drawings on the practice pages.

Practice pages- Remember we want to invoke speed!

Character Details

Now that you have become familiar with the basics of getting your character drawn and you feel confident with your practice, it is time to proceed to more advanced details .

Hands

Hands are one of the hardest things to create, especially when they are holding things or just standing there you really want those hands to look as natural as possible.

You saw at the beginning of the course that I did some simple hands on the exaggerated characters. This is a great way to get you started. We always want to break down a shape into smaller more manageable shapes. This is easier to manipulate the characters hands into various positions you would like. I always do a sketch layer before I do my final drawing.

Layers are your best friend when it comes to digital art and something you need to get used to. I am getting off topic. I will teach you more later about this but having things on separate layers in a drawing save you from having to redraw the whole thing if an error has occurred or your client asks for changes.

Here are the basics of a hand shape. *(See illustration on the next page).* I want you to just concentrate on working on hands now. Let us try to make several different hand positions and signs to get a feel for many hand movements and gestures. There are some children's books that avoid hands all together using only a thumb and then rounding the rest of the hand in a circle. It can be done, if necessary, but it is nice to be able to master this.

I made this image quickly to show you how you can draw this without having to sweat out the details. Once you get used to the shape of a hand in broken down form, it becomes easier to draw the outline of the hand once you have created a layer of circles using this method. This is a great way to get those tricky hands perfectly drawn every time.

"Believe that you can do it, cause you can do it."
— <u>Bob Ross</u>

Illustration example:

Always draw the palm first before fingers

Your Practice Exercise: Create your own different hand movements using the circle method shown. Breaking down the hand into shapes to help make it easier to draw hands correctly.

Practice pages:

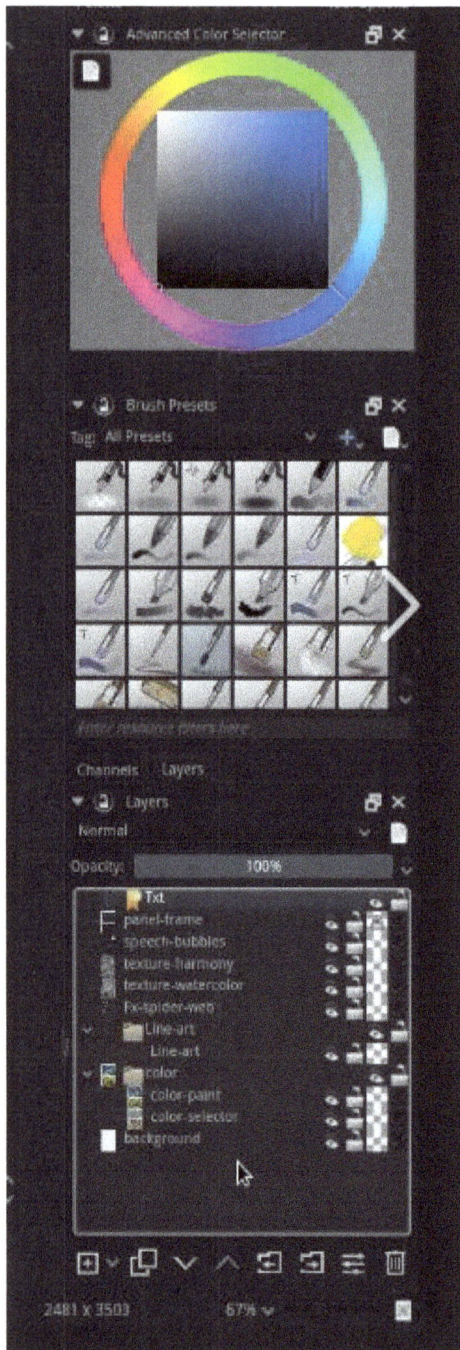

Layers for Digital Drawings

This **is crucial to your artwork if you are working on a digital drawing application**. This helps to avoid repetition or having to redo the whole image and saves time, which makes you a more effective illustrator.

Layers are your friend; these layers also need to be clearly labeled as you go. So, background image will always be what you first start with on any new drawing. Before you do anything else <mark>create a new layer</mark> and make sure that the resolution for your drawing is a minimum of **300 DPI**. This will ensure a crisp clear image for printing your image into a book.

Always label each layer, I cannot emphasis this enough, and separate your linework, and colour from the background.

Colour for character layer should be separate. You can even break that down even more if you wanted to. Let us say for example you are using a scene multiple times, simply remove the characters on top of those layers and save as a PDF as the background. This way you do not have to constantly recreate a new background one every time if the character is in one room or place. Characters you can also isolate on their own as well and you can save them individually in a file. You can then simply place them on top of your initial background image and modify the character accordingly on its own layer.

So, for example let us say a character has her hand up now pointing. You do not need to redraw the whole character you simply need to modify it by erasing the arm where it is and moving it upward with correct hand gestures. This makes for a much faster finished drawing then having to start from scratch again. This is not always the case sometimes when the character is now sitting. What you can do to maintain the standard of her face is simply using the quick selection tool copy and paste the face onto your new character to maintain the same shapes if you are concerned about consistency.

You can also change the opacity to 50% and create a new layer on top of the original so that you can position your face correctly using the layer underneath as a guide to help you recreate it with its added features. These are little tricks to help you to maintain consistency throughout the book..

Make sure you qet to know the program you are using, press all the buttons, watch YouTube videos and see how things work and function on your drawing application There are a lot of tricks that you can learn from watching other people work their magic. It's one thing to see it, but its quite an other to be hands on. Remember to practice so you know your application and it will make for faster illustrations in the end.

So dive right in, do not be scared. Everything can be deleted and then shut down and reopened if needed. These tools on your application are there to make your life easier, but you need to know them and have confidence in your application to do the job right.

Digital Art Practice Exercise: Utilize the program to create multiple layers and draw a single element on each layer to demonstrate how different components remain separated in an illustration.

This layering you are doing acts the same as panes of glass. You can see the whole picture but it remains separate whiich is perfect for you to change things as needed individually.

Once you get familiar with the layers you will understand how important it is to use them. You wont have to redraw the whole thing if only one object needs some adjustments, mainly character or background elements.

Shading

I am going to get away from the tech stuff and get to the complicated shading stuff.

Ok, with shading it can seem like a simple enough task depending on how you wish to illustrate your book. But there are some things that you need to take into consideration when dealing with shading. See illustration:

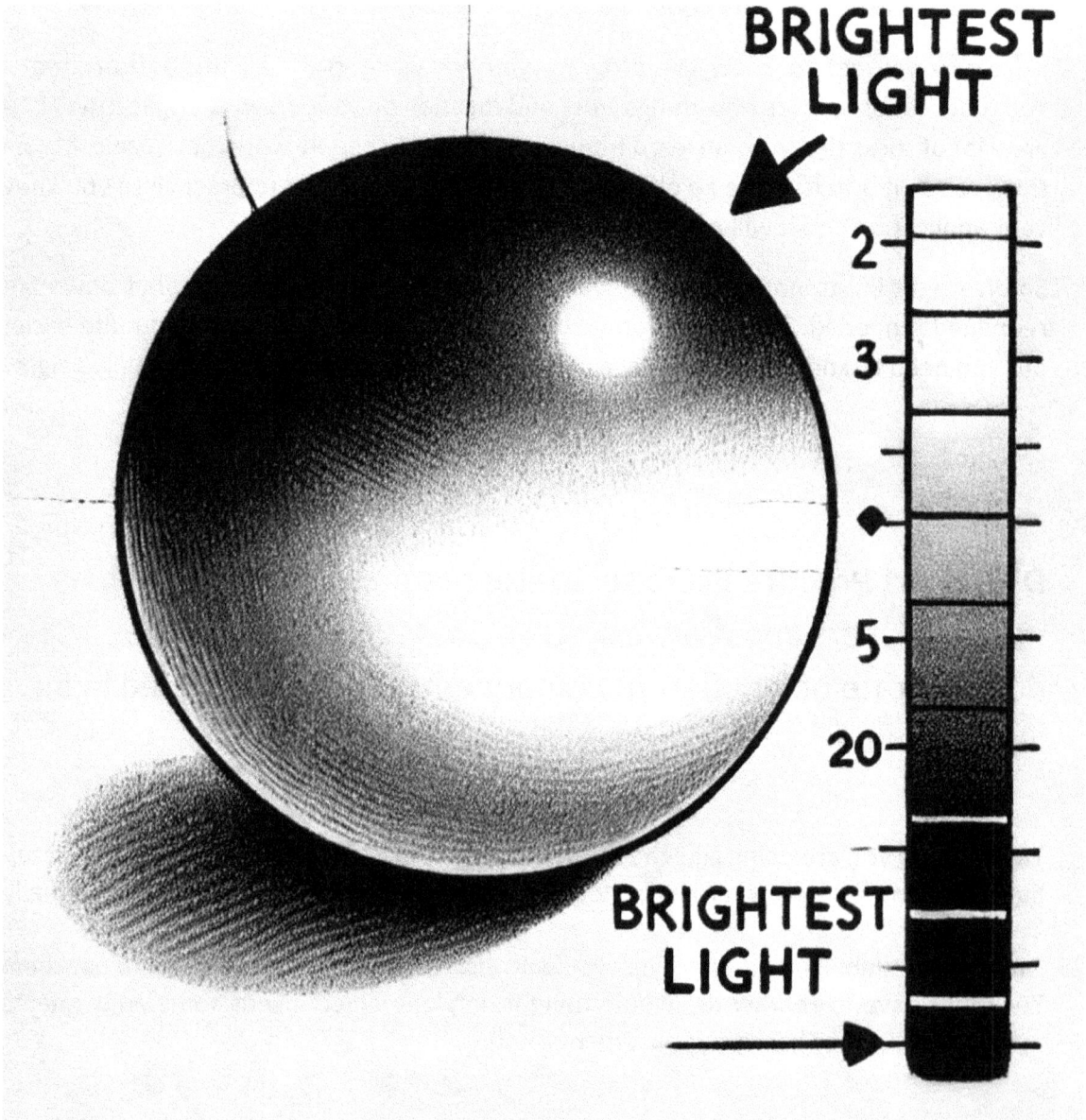

BRIGHTEST LIGHT

2-
3-

5-

20-

BRIGHTEST LIGHT

This next illustration looks worse than it is. Use this as your guide to help you realize the depth in which shading can really go to. There are always different grades to shading depending on where the light hits first and where the rest of it bounces off or even if it has texture. Ask yourself questions like, is the surface itself reflective in which the light bounces off, and so on.

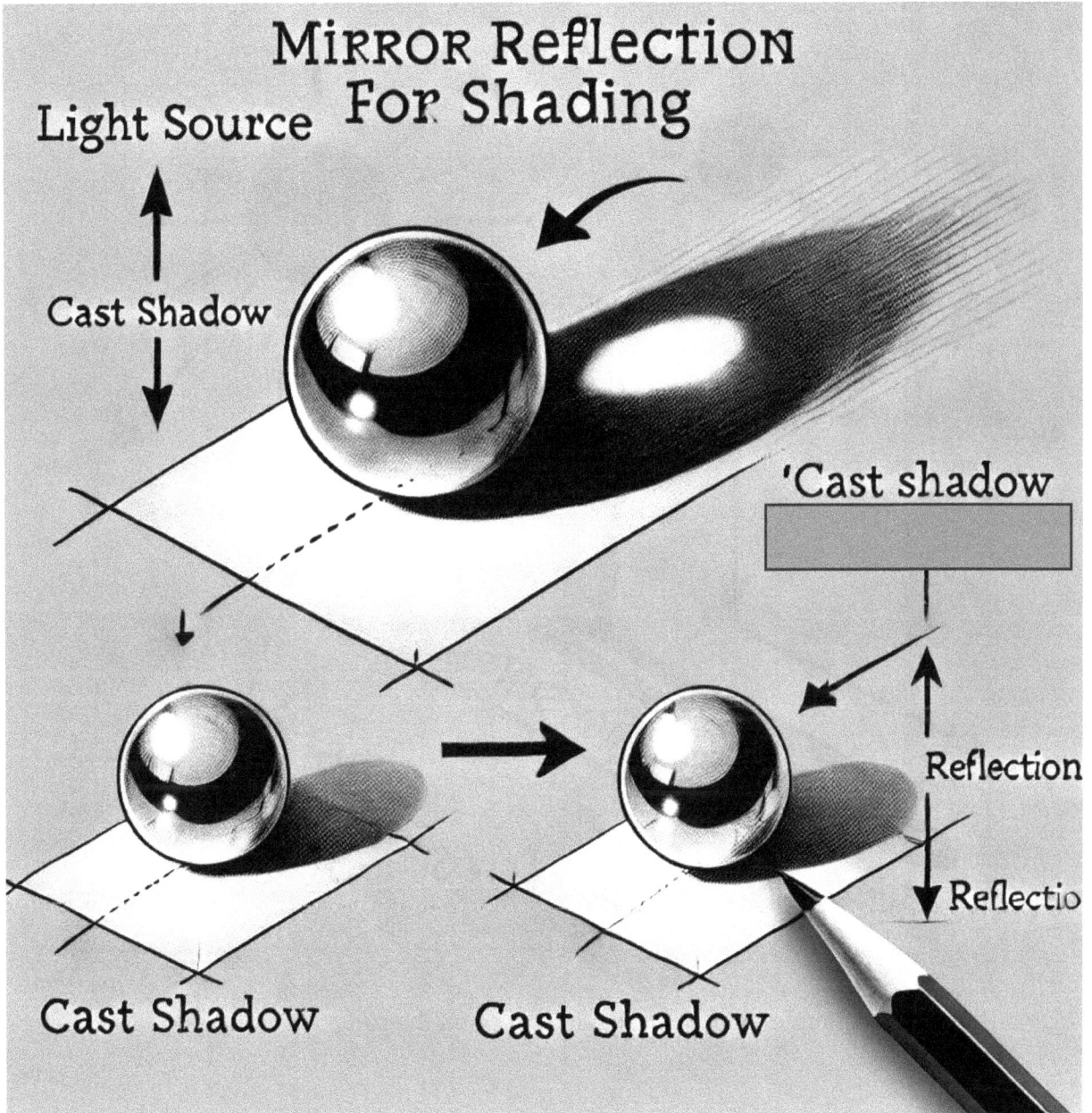

Something you should keep in mind when working with different surfaces. I would encourage you to look at some children's books to see different depths of details books have. Some have a lot, and some are quite simple yet very effective. This is your choice to decide how much or how little you want to show. These charts will help guide you to shading the right way according to the position of lights or sunlight showing depth to your drawing.

Here is also a simple example of shading based on the sun positioning.

Your Practice Exercise: Take a simple object like a circle or a square as shown in the examples and try to point the direction of the light using an arrow wherever you like. Then shade the rest of the circle gradually getting darker the farther away you get from the main source of light.

"Gotta have opposites, light and dark and dark and light, in painting. It's like in life. Gotta have a little sadness once in a while, so you know when the good times come. I'm waiting on the good times now." — **Bob Ross**

Practice pages

Understanding Hatching, Cross-Hatching, and Stippling for Depth & Shading

These techniques help you create depth, texture, and contrast without blending!

Hatching (*Parallel Lines*) is using closely spaced parallel lines to create shading. The closer the lines, the darker the area appears. The farther apart, the lighter it looks.

This technique is used for soft shadows, Light-to-dark gradients or simple textures *(fabric, smooth surfaces)*.

Hatching Technique

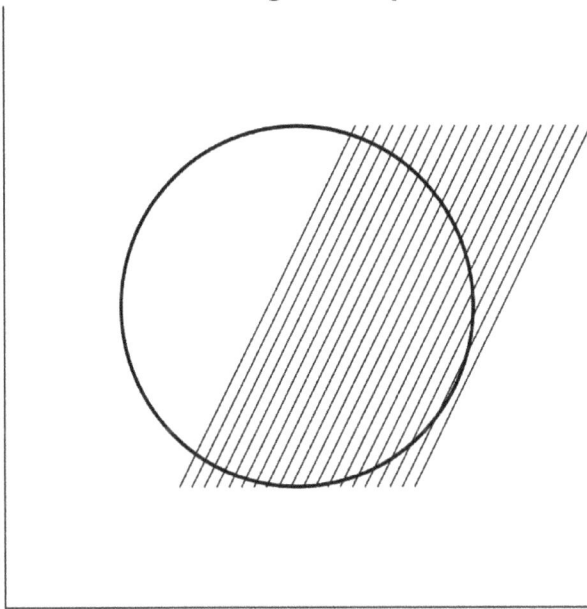

The lines should stay within the object, not as this illustration shows unless you are extending it to create a shadow..

Your Practice Exercise: Draw a sphere and use hatching to create light and shadow from one side to another. Try changing the line direction (vertical, diagonal, curved) to match the form.

Practice page:

Cross-Hatching (*Crisscrossing Lines*) is two or more layers of hatching overlapping at different angles. This Creates a richer, more detailed tonal range. More layers = darker shading.

This is great for stronger shadows, textures like wood grain or rough surfaces and high-contrast areas.

Cross-Hatching Technique

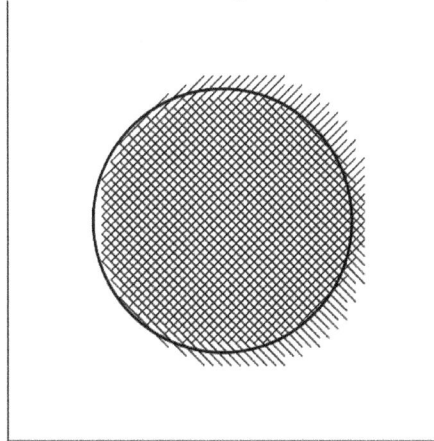

Your Practice Exercise: Draw a cube and shade each side differently: One with hatching One with cross-hatching and One left white to show the light source.

Practice Page:

Lastly, we have the **stippling technique** (*Dots for Shading)*. These are tiny dots placed close together that create a shaded effect. The denser the dots, the darker the shading. It is also great for soft, organic textures.

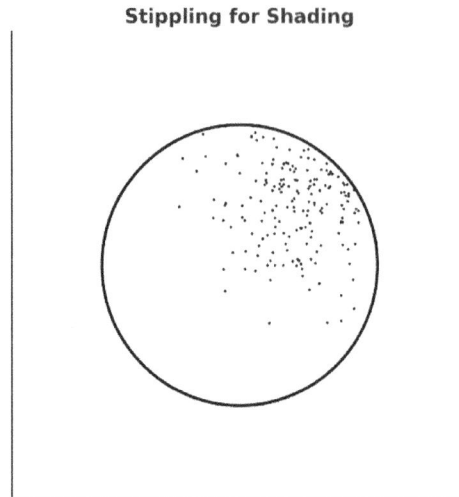

Stippling for Shading

This is best used For: Soft transitions (e.g., skin, clouds, mist) Fine detail work (e.g., freckles, fur, fabric) Textured surfaces (e.g., stone, sand, rough paper)

Your Practice Exercise: Draw a **circle** and shade it with only stippling. Try to use **light, medium, and heavy dot densities**.

Practice Page:

All right, now you are an expert at shading!

Character movements

I love to see full body characters running or walking, playing ball or simply standing. But it is not the easiest thing to do. There are a lot of things to consider. Body movement, positioning of legs and arms so they make sense to look at it. Here below is a character walking, notice how its arms and legs change positioning and looks exaggerated but natural. Practice using the circle shapes of the body to emulate some of the movements to really get a feel for how the characters is moving. Practice only with the shapes and slowly build up your character outline.

Here is an image to emphasize the character walking

This concept can be applied to an animal, but we must think of it in doubles. Here is an example of it in movement notice the way in which its body stretches and then shrinks back building up

the momentum for the next move, just like a spring loaded before it bounces.

Bodies can be fun to manipulate once you get the hang of it. Practice makes perfect. Remember talent is just a pursued interest in something!

Your Practice Exercise: Create your own character or animal using the examples shown to create movement. Use the circles technique to initiate the character before detailing it to ensure that the proportions are correct.

Practice Pages:

Understanding Backgrounds in Illustrations

There are **three layers of background**:
Foreground – Closest to the viewer, contains key objects/characters.
Middle Ground – Adds depth, includes supporting elements.
Background – Distant elements like sky, trees, or cityscapes.

Here is a visualization of foreground, middle ground, and background to visually see what I am talking about.

Illustration Depth: Foreground, Middle Ground, Background

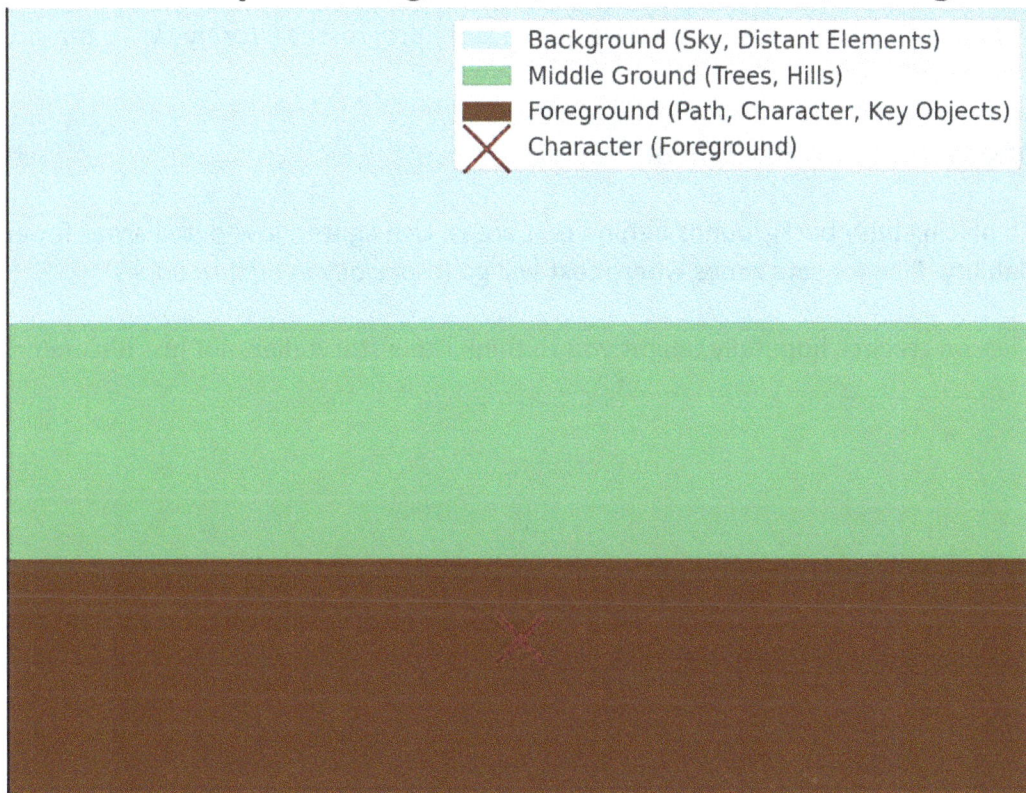

- Foreground (Brown) – Closest to the viewer, contains the main character and key objects.
- Middle Ground (Green) – Adds depth, includes supporting elements like trees or hills.
- Background (Blue) – The most distant elements, such as the sky, mountains, or far-away buildings.

The differences between simple vs. Detailed: Backgrounds shouldn't overpower the main characters. Blurry vs. Sharp: Important elements should be clearer, while distant elements can be faded or simplified. Use Negative Space Wisely: Don't overcrowd pages—leave space for text and visual balance.

For example, we want to use leading lines (paths, roads, fences) to guide the eye. Perhaps frame your characters using windows, doorways, or natural elements. I would encourage you to experiment with **angles** as discussed in our previous lessons.

Storytelling through background details add small details that hint at the story *(toys, books, weather changes)*. Use symbolism (*e.g., messy room = chaotic character, bright sun = hopeful*). Let backgrounds evolve as the story progresses (*stormy sky at the climax, tidy room at the end).*

Working with Text Placement

Avoid placing busy backgrounds behind text areas. Use lighter, low-detail areas for easy readability. Plan for safe zones where text will go (*especially in picture books*).

This lesson teaches hopefully taught you to think like a storyteller, not just illustrator.

Your Practice Exercise: Create a busy vs. simple background illustration using the three different layers of background, then place the text over top of it. This will show you that text is just as important as the illustration.

Practice Pages:

Character clothing

Clothing should always fit the story when choosing an appropriate design. You can have a lot of fun with this. But try not to take away too much from the character unless this is something you are trying to convey. The character who is quite silly can have a Hawaiian top on with a coconut bra on top. With extra-large glasses that does not fit his face and live in Florida for example would be appropriate and hilarious for kids and parents if its regarding something in that place and it is a comedy book.

So, it is up to you to decide the kind of outfit. Does the outfit correspond with the era? There is also something to think about all these intricate details will get your book illustrations looking amazing professional and will attract people to want to buy the book.

Your Practice Exercise: Create clothing using different eras in time. What are the common clothes of the 80's or even the 1800's. Research different eras to help get an accurate depiction of the clothes worn for that time period.

Practice pages:

The Art of Pen-Only Drawings

In this exercise I will help you develop critical thinking skills, intentional mark-making, and artistic confidence by drawing exclusively with only a pen.

Why Use Only a Pen? Forces you to think before you draw (no erasing). Develops hand control and confidence in line work. Encourages creative problem-solving when mistakes happen. Improves line weight variation, shading, and hatching skills.

Your Practice Exercises:

Start with these quick, stress-free warm-ups. Pick at least three of these exercises and draw them on the following practice pages.

Blind Contour Drawing

Choose an object, look only at the object, not the paper. Draw slowly in one continuous line, following the edges with your eyes. This builds hand-eye coordination and forces you to trust your marks.

Continuous Line Drawing

Pick a simple subject *(a hand, fruit, or a chair)*. Draw it without lifting the pen from the page. This helps with flow, confidence, and seeing connections between shapes.

Weighted Line Drawing

Practice drawing thick and thin lines by applying different pressure. This is great for creating depth and contrast in pen sketches.

The "Mistake-Friendly" Drawing

Draw any object or scene using a pen. If a mistake happens, turn it into something intentional (*add texture, modify a shape, integrate it into the drawing*). This exercise builds resilience and adaptability.

One-Minute Sketches

Set a timer for 1 minute per drawing. Sketch fast and loosely, focusing on capturing essence over detail. This is a fantastic way of building confidence and reducing overthinking.

Cross-Hatching & Texture *(check shading section)*

Draw a simple shape (*a cube, apple, or sphere*). Shade it only using hatching, cross-hatching, and stippling. Helps with depth and tonal values without relying on blending.

After finishing these exercises, analyze your work:

- What did you learn from drawing without an eraser?
- How did your thought process change?
- Which techniques (hatching, bold lines, planning ahead) felt most useful?

Practice Pages:

Storyboard basics

A storyboard is a visual plan for a book, showing how illustrations will flow from one page to the next. It helps illustrators organize their ideas, maintain consistency, and ensure the story progresses smoothly. And it will also help your author to visualize how you envision the book based on the text they have provided.

The Basic Structure of a Picture Book

- Picture books are usually 32 pages (standard format).
- The story always follows a structure: beginning, middle, and end.
- Each spread (two facing pages) should advance the story visually and emotionally. We can use a spread to emphasize a dramatic point in the story or something we want the reader to really see with a two-page spread illustration.

A Simple Grid Layout

Your Practice Exercise: Create a thumbnail storyboard using a grid of 8-16 small boxes on a sheet of paper on your own using the template shown to you.

Remember:

Each box represents a page or spread. This is your decision, or the decision of the author. You will be collaborating with them so make sure that you are both on the same page before you begin illustrating a final copy. Communication is paramount. Use rough sketches to plan the illustrations, focusing on composition and pacing rather than adding in details.

Children's Book Storyboard Template

Page 1	Page 2	Page 3	Page 4
Page 5	Page 6	Page 7	Page 8
Page 9	Page 10	Page 11	Page 12
Page 13	Page 14	Page 15	Page 16

How a story moves helps to create anticipation and should be planned carefully. Slow moments vs. fast-paced scenes, like we discussed. Remember to use different perspectives to create interest.

Storyboards should also leave room for text placement. We need to have balancing text and illustration ratio to avoid cluttered pages. So, we can decide right from the start if the author prefers text on one side and illustrations on another or whatever their preference is to avoid having to create many storyboards. For spread pages, you will be using text on an illustration so you must remember to leave an allowance for it.

Remember to Use Stick Figures & Rough Sketches First in Your Storyboard

Beginners often focus too much on details too early. Don't worry about this yet. Storyboarding is about planning, not perfect drawings.

Your Practice Exercise: Analyze Published Picture Books

Study real picture books and analyze how illustrators use storyboarding techniques. Ask yourself questions like: *How does the illustrator guide your eyes? How does the page turn affect the story? This will help you learn how to develop your eye skills and knowledge for when its time to create your own book.*

Storyboards do often go through multiple drafts. We need to remember to **step back, review, and adjust** the compositions for clarity and impact.

Now that you have all the basic drawing skills you need, let's help to educate you on the world of illustration in business, and what you need to succeed!

Helpful tips for entering the world of children's book illustrations

Diving into the world of children's book illustration, it's crucial to understand the market. The children's book industry is vast and diverse, with a wide range of genres and age groups. From picture books for toddlers to chapter books for older children, each category requires a different illustration style and approach. Research popular children's books, analyze their illustrations, and identify current trends in the industry. This knowledge will help you tailor your work to meet the demands of publishers and readers.

Identifying Your Target Audience

Knowing your target audience is essential for creating illustrations that resonate with readers. Consider the age group you want to focus on and study their preferences. Younger children may prefer bright, colorful, and simple illustrations, while older children might appreciate more detailed and sophisticated artwork. Understanding your audience will enable you to create illustrations that capture their imagination and hold their interest.

Developing Your Skills

To succeed as a children's book illustrator, you need to continuously hone your skills and stay updated with the latest techniques. Here are some key areas to focus on:

Mastering Different Styles

Children's book illustrations come in various styles, such as realistic, whimsical, cartoonish, and abstract. Experiment with different styles to find your unique voice and versatility. This will make you more appealing to a broader range of clients and projects.

Improving Your Drawing Techniques

Strong drawing skills are the foundation of successful illustrations. Practice regularly to improve your anatomy, composition, perspective, and use of color. Consider taking art classes or workshops to learn new techniques and receive constructive feedback.

Digital Illustration Skills

In today's digital age, proficiency in digital illustration tools like Adobe Illustrator, Photoshop, and Procreate is essential. These tools offer various features that can enhance your work and streamline your workflow.

Building a Portfolio

A well-curated portfolio is your ticket to landing illustration gigs. Your portfolio should highlight your best work and demonstrate your ability to illustrate children's books. Sites like Artstation or Behance are great places to have an online place to show your work. Here are some tips for creating a compelling portfolio:

Showcase a Variety of Work

Include a diverse range of illustrations that highlight your versatility. Feature different styles, characters, and settings to show potential clients that you can adapt to various projects.

Illustrate Sample Book Pages

Create sample illustrations for existing children's book texts or write your own short stories. This will give clients a clear idea of how you bring stories to life and manage different narrative elements.

Keep It Updated

Regularly update your portfolio with new work to reflect your growth and current skills. An up-to-date portfolio shows clients that you are active and continuously improving.

Finding Work

Once you have a strong portfolio, it's time to find work as a children's book illustrator. Here are some strategies to help you get started:

Networking

Networking is crucial in the illustration industry. Attend industry events, join online forums, and connect with authors, publishers, and fellow illustrators. Building relationships can lead to collaboration opportunities and referrals. Post your work on Facebook groups to show your art.

Submitting to Publishers

Research children's book publishers and submit your portfolio to those who accept unsolicited submissions. Follow their submission guidelines carefully and tailor your portfolio to match their preferred styles and themes.

Freelance Platforms

Join freelance platforms like Upwork, Fiverr, and Behance to find illustration gigs. These platforms allow you to display your work, bid on projects, and connect with potential clients.

Self-Publishing

Consider partnering with authors to self-publish children's books. Self-publishing offers more creative control and the potential for higher royalties. Platforms like Amazon Kindle Direct Publishing make it easier to publish and distribute your work if you have no experience yet.

Setting Your Rates

Determining your rates can be challenging, especially when you're starting. Research industry standards and consider factors like your experience, the complexity of the project, and the time required. Be transparent with clients about your rates and be open to negotiation. Remember to give a lower rate for the first few books to build your portfolio. Once you have a few under your belt feel free to raise your prices because you now have experience in the field and people who are willing to speak on your behalf. I would even encourage you to do one or two projects for free but ask that your name be on the front cover to show your name in a book. When you have a printed book with your name on it, this shows you have experience and can start charging fees.

Marketing Yourself

Effective marketing can help you stand out in a competitive market. Here are some strategies to promote yourself as a children's book illustrator:

Creating a Website

A professional website serves as your online portfolio and contact point. Include your best work, an about section, and contact information. Consider adding a blog to share your insights and experiences.

Utilizing Social Media

Social media platforms like Instagram, Twitter, and Pinterest are excellent for highlighting your work and connecting with your audience. Share your illustrations, behind-the-scenes content, and engage with your followers.

Collaborating with Authors

Forming collaborations with authors can lead to steady work and help you build a reputation in the industry. Reach out to authors whose work you admire and propose collaboration ideas.

Illustrating children's books is a fulfilling and lucrative career for those with a passion for art and storytelling. By understanding the market, developing your skills, building a strong portfolio, and effectively marketing yourself, you can turn your passion into a profitable profession. Embrace the journey, stay persistent, and let your creativity shine in every illustration you create.

YOU DID IT!!!!

Congratulations, you finished the course!

But Before you go!

Let's see what you have learned. IF at any point you do not remember some of the answers that means you may need to study or practice a little more! That is okay, this course is for practicing to perfect your craft so you can create stunning illustrations of your own.

QUESTIONS FOR RECAP

1.What is the most important thing when it comes to drawing?

_____

2.What is the easiest way to break down a full body?

_____

3.How do you make a character stand out above the rest?

_____

4.Eyes are the window of? How important are eyes in character drawings?

_____

5.How do you fully convey a character's emotions?

_____

6.When drawing different hand positions what is the rule of thumb?

_____

7.What is the first thing you do when opening a new file for drawing?

_____

8.How do you separate backgrounds from characters and any other items you want to contain in your illustrations?

_____

9.When it comes to shading, depending on this_____ will show where you put the shading.

_____

10.How often should you draw to grow your creative muscle?

_____

11.Based on textures, how will that affect the surrounding light?

_____

12.For creating movement in an illustration? What are two things that can create that?

_____

13.Full figure drawings are easiest if they are tackled by doing this?

_____

14.For animals we think of them as a spring which is dependent on what?

_____

15. Character clothing should reflect what?

_____

16. What is the unspoken rule of drawing?

_____

17. To get a dynamic character composition what is the rule to make one?

_____

18. When choosing color palettes, what do we need to decide first?

_____

19. What do people notice the most in an illustration? Is it color? Lines?

_____

20. What is the minimum resolution needed for an illustration?

_____

21. What is the best way to achieve an angled drawing?

_____

22. Why is practicing with pen only a great lesson for artists?

_____

23. What is stippling used for mainly?

_____

24. Why is setting your rates fairly based on experience as an illustrator so important?

_____

Thank you for taking the time to go over this beginner illustration course, we wanted to make it an easy pleasant experience giving you jam packed knowledge to carry you while you begin your journey in the world of illustrating.

REMEMBER it will not happen overnight. PRACTICE, PRACTICE, and then practice some more!

When you are ready, advertise on social media that you are now offering illustration services to get friends and family involved and even get a paid gig! Good luck, on your journey I hope I helped you gain practical skills and increased your confidence!

*ANY QUESTIONS PLEASE FEEL FREE TO EMAIL US AT
ELITELIZZARDPUBLISHING@HOTMAIL.COM

Answers to your question page:

1 Practice 2 Using the circles method 3 using the odd rule 4 Soul, invoke emotions and connection. 5 body posture 6 circle method 7 warm up doing quick circles and drawings and getting familiar with your tools. 8 by creating more than one layer in your drawing for digital artwork. 9 light positioning 10 every day 11 it will displace the light differently 12 blurring the illustration to show speed and character positioning 13 break down the body in a series of circles to ensure proper stance 14 how fast they are moving 15 the era 16 not using the same positioning from left to right of a character 17 odd number of objects in a illustration page 18 decide the feeling we are trying to convey 19 characters 20. 300 dpi 21. use a ruler and follow the lines of perspective 22. It teaches critical thinking skills 23. Skin and sand type illustrations 24. Because it leaves you transparent to clients and they will be more willing to work with you

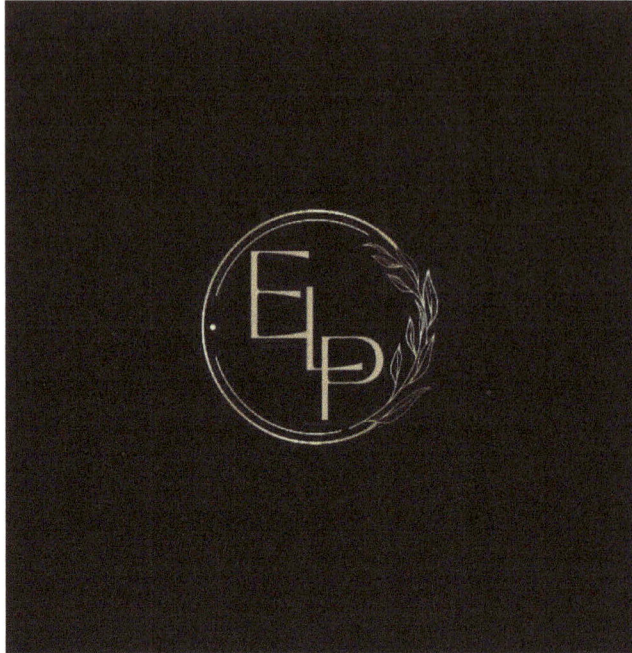

The Elite Lizzard Publishing Company is a Canadian book publisher dedicated to helping change the world one book at a time.